STAND

Your Weekly Guide for Success

Ruben Mata

Foreword by Dr. Cesar Vargas

WHAT OTHERS ARE SAYING…

"If you are ready to achieve a greater level of success and happiness, then read and use the strategies in this brilliant book by my friend Ruben Mata."

James Malinchak
Featured on ABC's Hit TV Show, "Secret Millionaire"
Co-Author, Chicken Soup for the College Soul
Founder, www.BigMoneySpeaker.com

"Just wanted to thank you for writing and sharing such an amazing book. My partner surprised me with it, because I've been depressed and will be going through my 7th back surgery soon. I started my first day three days ago; since then, I have really learned a lot, and you're absolutely right: It is not EASY, but it is worth the challenge. Thank you."

G.P.

"My estranged daughter and son are back in my life because I chose to live for ME and believe in Him that all things will come to me as I wait patiently. I have re-read your book and shared it with several friends and family. Ruben Mata saved me from my own silliness and helped me see that I AM valuable and can be as awesome as I allow myself to be. I'M FINALLY HAPPY! Love you for your kinds words and truth."

Gina Cortes

Editing & Formatting: Dr. Cesar Vargas

Cover Design: Cesar Vargas, Ph.D.

"All The Way to the Top" Publishing

11852 Santa Rosalia
Stanton, California 90680

ISBN 978-0-615-82798-8

www.**Stand**with**Ruben**.com

DEDICATION

This book is dedicated to my amazing Father, Pedro Mata, Sr. (RIP), and my awesome Mother, Frances Mata. I always remember our conversations about life with my parents. My Father said, "The day you think you know everything, something happens and you start learning something new, so always be willing to learn." My Mother is more of the compassionate one. She said, "*Mijo*, always do things in life with love, and remember to always keep your faith in God."

I am blessed and highly favored with my health, my family and having God in my life. There is nothing I would change. I love life and everything it has for me because I know it is with a purpose.

– Ruben Mata

ACKNOWLEDGEMENTS

There are many people I love to thank for being a part of my life and have supported me through my journey in going "All the Way to the Top".

My wife Jessica, for having the patience, faith and being supportive.

My Familia, Johnny, Florence, Martin, Pete Jr., Irene, Albert, Franny, Jessie, Jose, Jarod, Raymond, Vanessa, Jessica, Marcus and Stevie.

Michael Stevenson of Transform Destiny, Clinton Swaine, Andrew Pais, Catherine Biggers, Bob Donnell, Daniel Charlier, Luis Espada, Deanna Brown, Theresa Douillard, Tony Robbins, T. Harv Eker, Les Brown, Blair Singer, Danny Katoa, James Malinchak.

Familias Huizar, Saldaña, Cuevas, Esparza, Lopez, Gonzalez, Escalera, Luna, Mata, Topinio, Balon, Mendoza, Chaidez, Toscano, Jefferson, Guerra, Wolfs, Lujan, Campos, S.R.S.G., Leonor Martínez, Juan & Claudia Anguiano, Javier & Leti Gálvez.

Special thanks to Ladis Lopez, Jr., Richard Barrier, Diane Schwartz, Maria Ortiz, Litda Phu, Carlos Muniz, Robert Esparza, Henry Bravo, Hector and Leopoldina Mendoza.

Ann McIndoo, my Author's Coach, Cesar Vargas, Justin Sachs.

In case I missed you, all of you have a special place in my heart!

Oh yea, my Frida, aka Cachi Boom Boom ☺. She's my dog. Hahaha!

TABLE OF CONTENTS
&

FOREWORD
BY DR. CESAR VARGAS

I FIRST MET RUBEN DURING A TRAINING ONE SUMMER, and the first thing that stood out to me about him was his huge smile and extremely positive attitude. His vibrant energy was shared with everyone around him, and many reciprocated. Then I found him on Facebook, and all of the pictures I saw of him had his contagious grin (and his signature "All the Way to the Top" hand gesture).

To be honest, I didn't think anyone could be so genuinely cheerful and positive *all the time*, but Ruben quickly changed my mind about that. He is *The Real Deal*!

When you get the chance to get to know Ruben, you'll enjoy his warm and caring attitude, his passion for helping people, and, yes, his huge, contagious smile.

He has risen through his own life struggles, and found the inspiration to do so by looking inside for strength, courage, and the will to be more, do more, and share more. This book is the result.

You can take comfort in knowing that my friend Ruben practices what he preaches, and you are the beneficiary of the wisdom, faith and inspiration he has complied over the years, which he now shares with you in these pages.

Perhaps as you read these pages and Ruben's reflections, you'll feel as I did, like he's talking directly to you, speaking to your life situations and what you can do NOW to get past them, and into your New Life.

As I say in one of my recent books, *YOU are the Michelangelo of your own life, the David you're sculpting is YOU.*

Now is the time for you to get started sculpting the Masterpiece that is your life, one quote at a time… one reflection at a time… one day at a time. And it begins now!

The master sculptor sees what's underneath the block of marble, and simply chisels away at the rest. Get to work on YOU. Start chiseling!

Now is your turn… Enjoy your Journey, All the Way to the Top!

Cesar Vargas, Ph.D.
Doctor of Clinical Hypnotherapy
www.**YourLifeIsYourMasterpiece**.com

𝒯HE 𝒥ORMAT

THIS IS A WORKBOOK, WHICH MEANS IT REQUIRES an active commitment on your part in order to get the result you want.

Every week, you'll get a quote from me, as well as my reflection on that quote, thought, idea or inspiration, and how to apply it in your life for maximum impact.

In the daily lines that follow, write your impressions and your results from that day, as you apply the weekly quote to your daily life.

Just like in life, your results will be in direct proportion to your efforts.

Go play full out, and you'll start seeing the results in no time.

The *work* starts right now! Fill in today's date, and schedule in your agenda, planner, etc., 11 months from now, to order your next book, and do it all over again to see how you've progressed: _____

I'd like to hear from you. Please feel free to email me your comments and a summary of your progress to Ruben@rubenmata.com

$\mathcal{I}$NTRODUCTION

CONGRATULATIONS! YOU NOW HAVE IN YOUR HANDS THE MANUAL for success. As I realized along my journey, there are many factors to consider. One of the main factors when starting is to keep it basic.

Many times I would over think things, which would make it difficult to take action. Once I saw and realized how simple things were, I was able to write down my plan, and work my plan on a daily basis.

Taking action like you are doing now, and applying these basic principles you have here in this book, I became a millionaire in less than three years.

Yes, it's that simple!

It's a great feeling to hear people say, "That's the millionaire who gave his time and donated to our charity."

As you get started on your journey to success, read the weekly quote and ask yourself these basic questions: Why am I applying this in my life? What are the steps I'm going to take with this quote? How am I going to apply these basic steps in my day? How do I know I have accomplished my goals?

If you're saying to yourself, *this is a lot of work*, it's okay. I thought that same exact way. Then I remembered what one of my mentors told me, "If you want things to change in your life, change what you're doing."

So, I did. And the results always tell the truth.

I use these same principles you are applying today, which give me the confidence, courage, and compassion to STAND firm and move forward on a daily basis.

Let's get started!

WEEK 1

You've been gifted with life; live it now to the fullest. People may not understand your goal; it's OK. It's not for them; it's yours. Here are the three P's required for success: Patience, Persistence, and remaining Positive. Enjoy your positive outcomes. I am focused... Now!

Ruben Mata

Focus for the week is remaining patient, persistent and positive during your journey in obtaining your desired outcome. Remember, what people think of you is not for you to decide. Your choice now is to have success.

Monday: _____

_____

_____

_____

Tuesday: _____

_____

_____

_____

Wednesday: _____

_____

_____

_____

Thursday: _____

_____

_____

_____

Friday: _____

_____

_____

_____

Saturday/Week-In-Review: _____

_____

_____

_____

_____

_____

$\mathcal{W}$EEK 2

❡

Birds of a feather flock together. Be aware of who you surround yourself with, because you subconsciously pick up their habits, attitude and ways about life. Align yourself now with powerful people with whom you will learn and grow. This will contribute to your growth in all areas of life. I am aware... Now!

Ruben Mata

This week take inventory of the people with whom you surround yourself. You are the average of the five people with whom you associate. It's your choice to surround yourself with successful people.

Monday: _____

_____

_____

_____

Tuesday: _____

_____

_____

_____

Wednesday: _____

_____

_____

_____

Thursday: _____

_____

_____

_____

Friday: _____

_____

_____

_____

Saturday/Week-In-Review: _____

_____

_____

_____

_____

_____

WEEK 3

*Fear, limited vision and lack of self esteem will guarantee you failure.
Passion, laser focus and persistence will guarantee you success.
You have the power to choose now. I am successful... Now!*

Ruben Mata

You get what you think about, so think about what you want. This week clarify what you are passionate about, make a plan and take action all the way through the finish line.

Monday: _____

_____

_____

_____

Tuesday: _____

_____

_____

_____

Wednesday: _____

_____

_____

_____

Thursday: _____

_____

_____

_____

Friday: _____

_____

_____

_____

Saturday/Week-In-Review: _____

_____

_____

_____

_____

_____

WEEK 4

Evaluate consequences up front. Every decision you make has a consequence, good or bad. Turn away from any temptation now that may cause you to break your word or lose your self-respect. The one thing you possess that is more valuable than your life is your honor. I am focused... Now!

Ruben Mata

From this moment forward, take a minute before your decisions are made and ask, "Is this helping me or hurting me?" Structure a game plan this week and take action daily. Now, enjoy your positive results.

Monday: _____

_____

_____

_____

Tuesday: _____

_____

_____

_____

Wednesday: _____

_____

_____

_____

Thursday: _____

_____

_____

_____

Friday: _____

_____

_____

_____

Saturday/Week-In-Review: _____

_____

_____

_____

_____

_____

WEEK 5

❡

Everything in life is a choice. Where you are is a result of the choices you've made. If you desire change in your life, simply change now what you're doing. It's that simple. I align myself with positive people...Now!

Ruben Mata

Now that you desire change, keep it simple and change. Realize when you change 1% more positive each day, in 90 days you will be almost 100% more positive than you are now.

Monday: _____

_____

_____

_____

Tuesday: _____

_____

_____

_____

Wednesday: _____

_____

_____

_____

Thursday: _____

_____

_____

_____

Friday: _____

_____

_____

_____

Saturday/Week-In-Review: _____

_____

_____

_____

_____

_____

WEEK 6

It's not what they call you; it's what you answer to. When someone makes a negative remark about you, it's a reflection of what's going on in them at your expense. Cut the cord now and release the "Energy Vampires" from your path. I am liberated... Now!

Ruben Mata

This week, start to realize we possess the power to accept or reject what people say about us. If it helps, great! If not, release it and continue to move forward.

Monday: _____

_____

_____

_____

Tuesday: _____

_____

_____

_____

Wednesday: _____

_____

_____

_____

Thursday: _____

_____

_____

_____

Friday: _____

_____

_____

_____

Saturday/Week-In-Review: _____

_____

_____

_____

_____

_____

WEEK 7

Obstacles are necessary to build character and shape us into champions. It's not how hard you hit; it's about how hard you can get hit and keep moving forward. Remain focused now on your desired outcome and the need to look back will be gone. I am persistent…Now!

Ruben Mata

Understand there is a process taking place, and the results are amazing. Keep looking forward this week and you will receive your championship trophy, which is your success.

Monday: _____

_____

_____

_____

Tuesday: _____

_____

_____

_____

Wednesday: _____

_____

_____

_____

Thursday: _____

_____

_____

_____

Friday: _____

_____

_____

_____

Saturday/Week-In-Review: _____

_____

_____

_____

_____

_____

*W*EEK 8

Catch someone doing something right instead of doing something wrong. Pay less attention now to what you hear about someone, and more to what you can learn from them. You'll be surprised. I am aware... Now!

Ruben Mata

Many times we have high expectations for people, which make us focus on what they're not doing. This week focus on the positive in them, and how they affect our life.

Monday: _____

_____

_____

_____

Tuesday: _____

_____

_____

_____

Wednesday: _____

_____

_____

_____

Thursday: _____

_____

_____

_____

Friday: _____

_____

_____

_____

Saturday/Week-In-Review: _____

_____

_____

_____

_____

_____

WEEK 9

If that which you think about you bring about, and you have the power to choose, what is the reason you haven't received that which you truly deserve? Positive change now happens with a positive choice. I am clear and laser focused... Now!

Ruben Mata

We have power in our words and thoughts. Be aware, present and positive with your thoughts this week and you'll be amazed with your results.

Monday: _____

_____

_____

_____

Tuesday: _____

_____

_____

_____

Wednesday: _____

_____

_____

_____

Thursday: _____

_____

_____

_____

Friday: _____

_____

_____

_____

Saturday/Week-In-Review: _____

_____

_____

_____

_____

_____

WEEK 10

Living with fear, procrastination and low self-esteem in your life is like driving your car with the emergency brake on. It's OK to let go and release now these limiting beliefs; you will reach your desired outcome easily and effortlessly. I release my limitations...Now!

Ruben Mata

Realize what or who is holding you back and weighing you down. Release them this week and you'll feel lighter.

Monday: _____

_____

_____

_____

Tuesday: _____

_____

_____

_____

Wednesday: _____

_____

_____

_____

Thursday: _____

_____

_____

_____

Friday: _____

_____

_____

_____

Saturday/Week-In-Review: _____

_____

_____

_____

_____

_____

WEEK 11

Your attitude will determine your success or failure. It will either support you or keep you from obtaining your desired outcome. Change your attitude now. Retrain your brain with positive thoughts; it will increase your confidence and attract the positive around you. I am positive... Now!

Ruben Mata

Keep a healthy and positive attitude. You'll enjoy all your positive results throughout the week, and for years to come.

Monday: _____

_____

_____

_____

Tuesday: _____

_____

_____

_____

Wednesday: _____

_____

_____

_____

Thursday: _____

_____

_____

_____

Friday: _____

_____

_____

_____

Saturday/Week-In-Review: _____

_____

_____

_____

_____

_____

WEEK 12

Many times we react on impulse. Wisdom is listening when we feel we need to be talking. Shhhhh… less is more. Many times silence makes more noise than thunder. I am wise… Now!

Ruben Mata

This week notice the people you consider wise. Be aware of composure and how they react in challenging times. Model success; you deserve it.

Monday: _____

_____

_____

_____

_____

Tuesday: _____

_____

_____

_____

_____

Wednesday: _____

_____

_____

_____

Thursday: _____

_____

_____

_____

Friday: _____

_____

_____

_____

Saturday/Week-In-Review: _____

_____

_____

_____

_____

_____

WEEK 13

Understand that you cannot change people; they have the right to be who they are. Change the way in which you relate to them, and watch the magic happen. I am changing... Now!

Ruben Mata

Be more concerned this week with your actions, and change YOU. The rest will align up exactly as it's supposed to.

Monday: _____

_____

_____

_____

_____

Tuesday: _____

_____

_____

_____

Wednesday: _____

_____

_____

_____

Thursday: _____

_____

_____

_____

Friday: _____

_____

_____

_____

Saturday/Week-In-Review: _____

_____

_____

_____

_____

_____

WEEK 14

Stop complaining now about the things you're not willing to change in your life. Keep in mind that when change starts, there will be chaos. Having strong beliefs and holding your composure will drive you to reach your desired outcome. I am focused...Now!

Ruben Mata

This week stand firm; let your 'yes' be 'yes' and your 'no' be 'no' as you begin to take action on reaching your desired outcome.

Monday: _____

_____

_____

_____

Tuesday: _____

_____

_____

_____

_____

Wednesday: _____

_____

_____

_____

Thursday: _____

_____

_____

_____

Friday: _____

_____

_____

_____

Saturday/Week-In-Review: _____

_____

_____

_____

_____

_____

WEEK 15

There are two types of beliefs: limiting and empowering. The quality of your life depends on the quality of your thoughts. Be aware! Your thoughts become feelings, feelings lead to actions and actions lead to results. I am empowered... Now!

Ruben Mata

Have empowering beliefs this week, remove now the limiting ones and feel your self-confidence increase.

Monday: _____

_____

_____

_____

Tuesday: _____

_____

_____

_____

Wednesday: _____

_____

_____

_____

Thursday: _____

_____

_____

_____

Friday: _____

_____

_____

_____

Saturday/Week-In-Review: _____

_____

_____

_____

_____

_____

WEEK 16

Realize your purpose in life and the values necessary to perform it. Practice now those very values and—most importantly—be a product of your own conclusion. I have clarity... Now!

Ruben Mata

Values are what motivate us to take action. This week, realize what values you possess. Write them down and look at them every day in the morning and feel the power you have.

Monday: _____

_____

_____

_____

Tuesday: _____

_____

_____

_____

Wednesday: _____

_____

_____

_____

Thursday: _____

_____

_____

_____

Friday: _____

_____

_____

_____

Saturday/Week-In-Review: _____

_____

_____

_____

_____

_____

WEEK 17

Are you making an "out-of-court settlement" with your life to avoid confrontation, in order to receive what you truly deserve? Realize how valuable you are, and how far you've come. Move forward with strength, courage and confidence. Enjoy the positive results that are waiting for you. I am worthy... Now!

Ruben Mata

Realize how much value you possess and what you've accomplished. Now that you realize your value, take action with your plan this week.

Monday: _____

_____

_____

_____

Tuesday: _____

_____

_____

_____

_____

Wednesday: _____

_____

_____

_____

Thursday: _____

_____

_____

_____

Friday: _____

_____

_____

_____

Saturday/Week-In-Review: _____

_____

_____

_____

_____

_____

WEEK 18

Pay your dues with integrity because everything matters. What goes around comes around; you can pay now, or pay double later. The quality of a person is not only what they do; it's also what they don't do to reach their desired outcome. I am at peace... Now!

Ruben Mata

This week, remember that you are always being watched. You know yourself better than anyone. Take 30 seconds to look in the mirror, and enjoy your reflection of you.

Monday: _____

_____

_____

_____

Tuesday: _____

_____

_____

_____

Wednesday: _____

_____

_____

_____

Thursday: _____

_____

_____

_____

Friday: _____

_____

_____

_____

Saturday/Week-In-Review: _____

_____

_____

_____

_____

_____

WEEK 19

Be aware, for there are many wolves dressed in sheep's clothing. Sincerity is not a test of truth. Think twice before you say, "He's so right because he is so sincere." Identify who you truly are, and you'll begin to see things more clearly. I am true to myself... Now!

Ruben Mata

This week, be aware of people's body language when they speak with you. Understand that communication is only 7% the words that people use, and 93% is comprised of body language and tonality.

Monday: _____

_____

_____

_____

Tuesday: _____

_____

_____

_____

Wednesday: _____

_____

_____

_____

Thursday: _____

_____

_____

_____

Friday: _____

_____

_____

_____

Saturday/Week-In-Review: _____

_____

_____

_____

_____

_____

WEEK 20

Accept it. Take ownership. It is what it is and move on. Avoid now the silly game of self-pity and playing the victim; it will threaten your future success. I am responsible for my life... Now!

Ruben Mata

Take ownership for your circumstances and realize how you are at cause for your situation. Once that happens you'll realize change is simple.

Monday: _____

_____

_____

_____

_____

Tuesday: _____

_____

_____

_____

_____

Wednesday: _____

_____

_____

_____

Thursday: _____

_____

_____

_____

Friday: _____

_____

_____

_____

Saturday/Week-In-Review: _____

_____

_____

_____

_____

WEEK 21

Today operate out of your vision instead of your past mindset of "Oh well; it has to be this way." Take action now on making that amazing, larger vision of yourself a reality. Allow the process to happen; it's easier than you think.

Ruben Mata

This week, decide what your larger vision is. Out with the old; in with the new. Become greater that you already are.

Monday: _____

_____

_____

_____

_____

Tuesday: _____

_____

_____

_____

Wednesday: _____

_____

_____

_____

Thursday: _____

_____

_____

_____

Friday: _____

_____

_____

_____

Saturday/Week-In-Review: _____

_____

_____

_____

_____

_____

ⱲEEK 22

What is your struggle that holds you down and has you feeling less than? Break those chains now! You see, true freedom is saying, "I no longer allow that in my life." I am liberated... Now!

Ruben Mata

This week, realize what your limitation looks like. No longer invest energy in that which doesn't serve you. You are feeling better now as you're reading.

Monday: _____

_____

_____

_____

Tuesday: _____

_____

_____

_____

Wednesday: _____

_____

_____

_____

Thursday: _____

_____

_____

_____

Friday: _____

_____

_____

_____

Saturday/Week-In-Review: _____

_____

_____

_____

_____

_____

WEEK 23

It's not about what people do or don't do. It's about how you respond and whether you choose to continue your life under these conditions. The quality of your life—or its lack of quality—depends on your choices. I choose the positive... Now!

Ruben Mata

People will do what they will and, at times, you may disagree. This week, take a minute and think of how wise you're becoming and what better choices you will make.

Monday: _____

_____

_____

_____

Tuesday: _____

_____

_____

_____

Wednesday: _____

_____

_____

_____

Thursday: _____

_____

_____

_____

Friday: _____

_____

_____

_____

Saturday/Week-In-Review: _____

_____

_____

_____

_____

_____

$\mathcal{W}$EEK 24

☞

It's funny how people enjoy your company, confidence and charisma until their ego takes over, then jealously and envy become their driving force. Set boundaries, remain focused and continue to move toward your desired outcome. I am aware...
Now!

Ruben Mata

Be aware of who you have in your environment. Now that you set boundaries in your life, realize who supports you and who is in your way. Eliminate the ones who are in your way and continue moving forward.

Monday: _____

_____

_____

_____

Tuesday: _____

_____

_____

_____

Wednesday: _____

_____

_____

_____

Thursday: _____

_____

_____

_____

Friday: _____

_____

_____

_____

Saturday/Week-In-Review: _____

_____

_____

_____

_____

_____

WEEK 25

If the messenger of misery stopped by to interrupt your flow it's OK you got this. Understand now you have the power and dominion over any situation you encounter because you are blessed and highly favored. I am victorious... Now!

Ruben Mata

The power you possess is amazing. This week, understand when problems come you can use your powerful confidence, and you will be victorious.

Monday: _____

_____

_____

_____

Tuesday: _____

_____

_____

_____

Wednesday: _____

_____

_____

_____

Thursday: _____

_____

_____

_____

Friday: _____

_____

_____

_____

Saturday/Week-In-Review: _____

_____

_____

_____

_____

_____

WEEK 26

Realize the positive changes in your life now that you decided to stretch, and break out of your comfort zone. Enjoy the feeling now that you're on the other side. I am powerful... Now!

Ruben Mata

This week, what comfort zones are you breaking through and have the powerful feeling of victory?

Monday: _____

_____

_____

_____

_____

Tuesday: _____

_____

_____

_____

_____

Wednesday: _____

_____

_____

_____

Thursday: _____

_____

_____

_____

Friday: _____

_____

_____

_____

Saturday/Week-In-Review: _____

_____

_____

_____

_____

_____

WEEK 27

Is now the day you say, "I'm ready for change; I'm tired of being sick and tired!"? Where you are this moment is a reflection of who you are inside. Be honest with yourself, not only when it's convenient, because it's a slow fade into the "gray zone" of settling for just enough to get by. Change your mindset and things will begin to change around you. I have a positive mindset…Now!

Ruben Mata

This week is the week for change! How will you stay outside the gray zone and enjoy the positive things around you?

Monday: _____

_____

_____

_____

Tuesday: _____

_____

_____

_____

Wednesday: _____

_____

_____

_____

Thursday: _____

_____

_____

_____

Friday: _____

_____

_____

_____

Saturday/Week-In-Review: _____

_____

_____

_____

_____

_____

WEEK 28

Are you living your life by design saying, "This is where I'm going," or by default: "This is what I'm settling for?" Order exactly what you desire from the menu of life, and you will receive it or remain in "the comfort zone" and settle for the leftovers. I design my life... Now!

Ruben Mata

This week, design your menu of life. Choose exactly what you're going to order and have. Enjoy your "Menu for Success."

Monday: _____

_____

_____

_____

_____

Tuesday: _____

_____

_____

_____

Wednesday: _____

_____

_____

_____

Thursday: _____

_____

_____

_____

Friday: _____

_____

_____

_____

Saturday/Week-In-Review: _____

_____

_____

_____

_____

WEEK 29

Remember: Before making a decision, evaluate consequences up front. Understand that when your emotions are up, your intelligence goes down; and when intelligence is up, your emotions go down. Every decision you make has a consequence, good or bad. I make intelligent decisions... Now!

Ruben Mata

When you make decisions this week, take a deep breath and think about your decision. You will be amazed of how different your positive results will be.

Monday: _____

_____

_____

_____

Tuesday: _____

_____

_____

_____

Wednesday: _____

_____

_____

_____

Thursday: _____

_____

_____

_____

Friday: _____

_____

_____

_____

Saturday/Week-In-Review: _____

_____

_____

_____

_____

_____

WEEK 30

Realize your purpose in life and the values necessary to perform it. Practice those very values and—most importantly—be a product of your own conclusion. I have clarity... Now!

Ruben Mata

This week, identify your values and what you're passionate about. Practice those positive values on a daily basis and watch the smile on your face and everyone around you.

Monday: _____

_____

_____

_____

Tuesday: _____

_____

_____

_____

Wednesday: _____

_____

_____

_____

Thursday: _____

_____

_____

_____

Friday: _____

_____

_____

_____

Saturday/Week-In-Review: _____

_____

_____

_____

_____

_____

WEEK 31

Everything you have in life is an expression of your level of awareness; when you lack it, you miss opportunity. Expand your level and you'll be surprised with your positive results. Enjoy your experience. I am aware... Now!

Ruben Mata

This week, be aware of your surroundings and be present when talking with people. Many times, opportunity is right in front of us.

Monday: _____

_____

_____

_____

Tuesday: _____

_____

_____

_____

Wednesday: _____

_____

_____

_____

Thursday: _____

_____

_____

_____

Friday: _____

_____

_____

_____

Saturday/Week-In-Review: _____

_____

_____

_____

_____

_____

WEEK 32

Never be afraid to expose a weakness in you. It may be challenging at first because we are not used to this type of mindset. Understand that accepting a weakness is the beginning of strength, and is the process of "The breakdown before the break through." I am strong... Now!

Ruben Mata

Positive change is happening now because you're looking and feeling different. What other weaknesses are you going to leave behind this week?

Monday: _____

_____

_____

_____

_____

Tuesday: _____

_____

_____

_____

Wednesday: _____

_____

_____

_____

Thursday: _____

_____

_____

_____

Friday: _____

_____

_____

_____

Saturday/Week-In-Review: _____

_____

_____

_____

_____

_____

WEEK 33

What dialogue do you listen to in the morning, words with fear and doubt or words with certainty and confidence? Remember, what we think about we bring about. Face your daily challenges with a certainty mindset, and enjoy the feeling as you watch them fall to the wayside. I am certain... Now!

Ruben Mata

The little voice we hear in our mind is powerful. It will help you or hurt you. This week manage the little voice, you now have the power.

Monday: _____

_____

_____

_____

Tuesday: _____

_____

_____

_____

Wednesday: _____

_____

_____

_____

Thursday: _____

_____

_____

_____

Friday: _____

_____

_____

_____

Saturday/Week-In-Review: _____

_____

_____

_____

_____

_____

WEEK 34

Feelings of anger, sadness, fear, hurt, and guilt are symptoms of an internal problem. "Band-aiding" them with an outside source is temporary. True change happens from the inside out. Ask and you shall receive; believe it then you'll see it. I am receiving... Now!

Ruben Mata

Realize the root cause of the problems you are overcoming this week. When you have a natural high, you'll know it because it's 100% you!

Monday: _____

_____

_____

_____

Tuesday: _____

_____

_____

_____

Wednesday: _____

_____

_____

_____

Thursday: _____

_____

_____

_____

Friday: _____

_____

_____

_____

Saturday/Week-In-Review: _____

_____

_____

_____

_____

_____

WEEK 35

Be aware that your earlier success can be your biggest liability. Refrain from the diluted belief that what you're doing is the only way. Always remain coachable. Remember, the mind is like a parachute: It works best when it's open. I am coachable...
Now!

Ruben Mata

This week, remember your biggest successes and what mindset you used to achieve those victories. Remain coachable and you are destined for greatness.

Monday: _____

_____

_____

_____

Tuesday: _____

_____

_____

_____

Wednesday: _____

_____

_____

_____

Thursday: _____

_____

_____

_____

Friday: _____

_____

_____

_____

Saturday/Week-In-Review: _____

_____

_____

_____

_____

_____

WEEK 36

Someone's opinion of you does not have to become your reality. What others say about you is none of your business. Be aware, mediocre-minded individuals want you down to their level. Set boundaries now; watch them fall to the wayside. I am confident... Now!

Ruben Mata

This week, eliminate the need of approval from others. Set and enforce boundaries in your life and feel the stress disappear, along with the energy drainers.

Monday: _____

_____

_____

_____

Tuesday: _____

_____

_____

_____

Wednesday: _____

_____

_____

_____

Thursday: _____

_____

_____

_____

Friday: _____

_____

_____

_____

Saturday/Week-In-Review: _____

_____

_____

_____

_____

_____

WEEK 37

Define who you are and your desired outcome; it will eliminate the feeling of doubt by the opinions of others. Insecure and wavering people will be frightened by anyone who directly or indirectly threatens their belief system. I have clarity... Now!

Ruben Mata

Clarity and being laser-focused will give you the power needed to reach your desired outcome. This week is set for cleaning the lenses and to take action!

Monday: _____

_____

_____

_____

_____

Tuesday: _____

_____

_____

_____

Wednesday: _____

_____

_____

_____

Thursday: _____

_____

_____

_____

Friday: _____

_____

_____

_____

Saturday/Week-In-Review: _____

_____

_____

_____

_____

WEEK 38

It takes more courage to accept insecurities than to deny them. I'm so grateful for my challenges that He has allowed me to go through because they make me who I am today. I am grateful... Now!

Ruben Mata

This week, realize the challenges you've overcome. Be aware of who you've become as a result of your victories.

Monday: _____

_____

_____

_____

_____

Tuesday: _____

_____

_____

_____

Wednesday: _____

_____

_____

_____

Thursday: _____

_____

_____

_____

Friday: _____

_____

_____

_____

Saturday/Week-In-Review: _____

_____

_____

_____

_____

WEEK 39

Do you feel the need to live an "airbrushed" lifestyle to impress others? Release the need and you will have true freedom. I am true to myself... Now!

Ruben Mata

Identify what style of life you're living. Is it to please others or you? This week, plan a daily goal being true to yourself.

Monday: _____

_____

_____

_____

_____

Tuesday: _____

_____

_____

_____

_____

Wednesday: _____

_____

_____

_____

Thursday: _____

_____

_____

_____

Friday: _____

_____

_____

_____

Saturday/Week-In-Review: _____

_____

_____

_____

_____

_____

WEEK 40

Until you forgive you are going backwards. Forgiving people now is for your benefit, not theirs. It's for you to move forward at a faster pace and receive what you truly deserve. I am a forgiving person...Now!

Ruben Mata

Identify the negative feelings you're carrying around from not being forgiving. This week, set up a schedule to forgive the people necessary, and you will feel positive and liberated!

Monday: _____

_____

_____

_____

Tuesday: _____

_____

_____

_____

Wednesday: _____

_____

_____

_____

Thursday: _____

_____

_____

_____

Friday: _____

_____

_____

_____

Saturday/Week-In-Review: _____

_____

_____

_____

_____

WEEK 41

Great leaders know when to display emotions and when to delay them. They ask, "What does the team need?" instead of, "What will make me feel better?" Mismanaging your emotions will cause people to fallback from you, instead of follow you. Teamwork makes the dream work! I am a great leader... Now!

Ruben Mata

You are a great leader. TEAM work makes the dream work. Communicate with your team regularly; it avoids a lot of assumptions; you'll be glad you did.

Monday: _____

_____

_____

_____

Tuesday: _____

_____

_____

_____

Wednesday: _____

_____

_____

_____

Thursday: _____

_____

_____

_____

Friday: _____

_____

_____

_____

Saturday/Week-In-Review: _____

_____

_____

_____

_____

_____

WEEK 42

Success is something you attract by becoming an attractive person... Positive = Attractive; Negative = Unattractive. Choose now and be positive throughout your day. I am positive... Now!

Ruben Mata

Success is a simple decision. This week, focus on remaining positive and identify the positive results.

Monday: _____

_____

_____

_____

_____

Tuesday: _____

_____

_____

_____

Wednesday: _____

_____

_____

_____

Thursday: _____

_____

_____

_____

Friday: _____

_____

_____

_____

Saturday/Week-In-Review: _____

_____

_____

_____

_____

_____

WEEK 43

Before the beginning of a great journey, there will be chaos. There are things that we never want to let go of. Keep in mind that letting go isn't the end of the world; it's now the beginning of a new life. I am liberated...Now!

Ruben Mata

This week, decide on your journey, and decide what you are letting go of, and leaving behind. Enjoy your positive results.

Monday: _____

_____

_____

_____

Tuesday: _____

_____

_____

_____

Wednesday: _____

_____

_____

_____

Thursday: _____

_____

_____

_____

Friday: _____

_____

_____

_____

Saturday/Week-In-Review: _____

_____

_____

_____

_____

_____

WEEK 44

Think positive thoughts; it will strengthen your confidence and you will take control of your life. The quality of one's life depends on one's thoughts. Because thoughts become feelings, feelings lead to actions, actions lead to results. I am positive...Now!

Ruben Mata

Design your mindset for success. It's simple to think positive thoughts. Plan this week for change and enjoy your new mindset.

Monday: _____

_____

_____

_____

Tuesday: _____

_____

_____

_____

Wednesday: _____

_____

_____

_____

Thursday: _____

_____

_____

_____

Friday: _____

_____

_____

_____

Saturday/Week-In-Review: _____

_____

_____

_____

_____

_____

WEEK 45

It takes more courage to apologize than not to. It takes more strength to relate to people than to dominate them. You don't have to pretend to be something you're not. Be true to yourself and improve in those areas. I am courageous...Now!

Ruben Mata

Be aware of how you talk with people. Being humble will lead to greater things when you identify who you truly are. Only then you'll realize you're a Super Star!

Monday: _____

_____

_____

_____

Tuesday: _____

_____

_____

_____

Wednesday: _____

_____

_____

_____

Thursday: _____

_____

_____

_____

Friday: _____

_____

_____

_____

Saturday/Week-In-Review: _____

_____

_____

_____

_____

_____

WEEK 46

When people make negative remarks about you, it's a reflection of what's going on in them at your expense. Life will test you; many people will criticize you to boost their own ego. Remain focused and you will reach your desired outcome. I am persistent... Now!

Ruben Mata

Remember that rejection is never personal. Remain positive and be present when the tests come, and remember it's their issue, not yours.

Monday: _____

_____

_____

_____

_____

Tuesday: _____

_____

_____

_____

Wednesday: _____

_____

_____

_____

Thursday: _____

_____

_____

_____

Friday: _____

_____

_____

_____

Saturday/Week-In-Review: _____

_____

_____

_____

_____

_____

WEEK 47

Be honest with yourself. Where can you improve more maturely than you have in the past? Successful people surround themselves with people who will confront them in areas in which they need to improve, that will help them grow and prosper. I am in a successful environment...Now!

Ruben Mata

This week, focus on your past and how things will be better in the future. Be aware of who you associate with. Are they helping you or hurting you?

Monday: _____

_____

_____

_____

Tuesday: _____

_____

_____

_____

Wednesday: _____

_____

_____

_____

Thursday: _____

_____

_____

_____

Friday: _____

_____

_____

_____

Saturday/Week-In-Review: _____

_____

_____

_____

_____

_____

WEEK 48

Pressure can make you or break you. Remember, there is a process taking place, and everything has a purpose. The only difference between a piece of black coal and a priceless diamond is the pressure it has endured. Hang in there and you will shine brighter than you've ever dreamed possible. I am strong...Now!

Ruben Mata

Understand that everything of value goes through a process. This week, focus on your value and how much you've overcome. You are champion!

Monday: _____

_____

_____

_____

_____

Tuesday: _____

_____

_____

_____

Wednesday: _____

_____

_____

_____

Thursday: _____

_____

_____

_____

Friday: _____

_____

_____

_____

Saturday/Week-In-Review: _____

_____

_____

_____

_____

WEEK 49

❦

Imagine a picture of your desired outcome (goal). See yourself living as if it already happened. How do you feel? What do you hear? And, what are you saying? Enjoy those emotions; they're yours and only yours! I am successful... Now!

Ruben Mata

This is a simple exercise you'll perform every day this week, and continue in the future. You will be amazed with your positive results.

Monday: _____

_____

_____

_____

Tuesday: _____

_____

_____

_____

Wednesday: _____

_____

_____

_____

Thursday: _____

_____

_____

_____

Friday: _____

_____

_____

_____

Saturday/Week-In-Review: _____

_____

_____

_____

_____

_____

$\mathcal{W}$EEK 50

Great leaders have many great qualities. Having strong beliefs and holding your composure now through popular and unpopular times is the most important characteristic of a great leader. I am a great leader... Now!

Ruben Mata

Be true to yourself. Hold strong to your values, for these are what drive and motivate us. You are a born leader!

Monday: _____

_____

_____

_____

_____

Tuesday: _____

_____

_____

_____

Wednesday: _____

_____

_____

_____

Thursday: _____

_____

_____

_____

Friday: _____

_____

_____

_____

Saturday/Week-In-Review: _____

_____

_____

_____

_____

WEEK 51

The only opinion that truly matters is our own. Other people's opinions are their thoughts, processed through their mental filters, which then become their results. Remember that nothing has meaning, only the meaning you give it. I control my life... Now!

Ruben Mata

Your opinion of your self is the only one that matters. Other people may want to bring you down. It's OK. Remain confident, and own your personal place of power.

Monday: _____

_____

_____

_____

Tuesday: _____

_____

_____

_____

Wednesday: _____

_____

_____

_____

Thursday: _____

_____

_____

_____

Friday: _____

_____

_____

_____

Saturday/Week-In-Review: _____

_____

_____

_____

_____

WEEK 52

Think about the people you have most loved or admired. What qualities moved you to feel affection or admiration towards them? Today, apply those same qualities that move you to your loved ones, for tomorrow may be too late.

Ruben Mata

This week, make a list of the people you most love, and how they impact your life. Apply those same qualities to others.

Monday: _____

_____

_____

_____

_____

Tuesday: _____

_____

_____

_____

Wednesday: _____

_____

_____

_____

Thursday: _____

_____

_____

_____

Friday: _____

_____

_____

_____

Saturday/Week-In-Review: _____

_____

_____

_____

_____

_____

About The Author

ൄ

RUBEN MATA HAS BEEN SHARING HIS PASSION of personal development for more than 7 years, and has been an international speaker for about half a decade, presenting a wealth of techniques and strategies for developing and empowering leaders.

As a Master Trainer, Success Coach, Author and Expert in success mindset, Ruben shows and teaches his audiences how to create a new mindset around success, prosperity, wealth and abundance.

Many people ask what is "All the Way to the Top". Here is the answer, in Ruben's own words: "In everything I do—be it in my spiritual walk, spending time with family or in business—I do things to the maximum of my ability which takes me 'All the Way to the Top!' I've developed a business model that helps people excel in all areas of their life, including mind, body and spirit, by having this 'All the Way to the Top' mindset I've created."

You can contact Ruben directly at ruben@rubenmata.com.

Made in the USA
San Bernardino, CA
21 November 2014